Rievaulx Abbey

Peter Fergusson, Glyn Coppack, Stuart Harrison
and Michael Carter

CONTENTS

Tour of the Abbey

THE CHURCH

Monastic churches usually have an east–west alignment. At Rievaulx the lie of the land did not allow for this, and the church is aligned from south-east to north-west. Conventionally, however, Rievaulx's buildings have been described as if having an east–west axis, and this guide does the same.

The church lay at the centre of monastic life, and served two distinct communities. The eastern half was used by the monks, who spent about five hours a day in their choir, maintaining a round of eight services and hearing Mass. The *Rule of St Benedict*, written in the 540s, which had come to form the basis for monastic life across western Europe, describes this responsibility as the *opus Dei*, the work of God, and it combined praise, thanksgiving and prayer. The western parts of the church served the lay brothers – the class of men who lived as part of the monastic community and whose heavier manual work underlay the monastic economy. They used the church twice a day for about one hour. Unlike the choir monks who could read and write, the lay brothers were mostly illiterate. They observed their own statutes, the *Usus conversorum*, which regulated their daily lives.

There is evidence of two main periods of building in the abbey church. The darker stone and simpler forms of the nave represent the older church, constructed in the late 1140s and now heavily ruined. Remains of a still earlier church, which the first monks here used, have been identified under the grass in the cloister. Beyond are the much more complete remains of a large eastern extension to the church built by about 1230. This work can be distinguished by a lighter coloured limestone, high-quality ashlar or squared stone, greater height and more elaborate forms.

Above: Fragment of an angel sculpture, possibly from a late 13th-century tomb
Left: View of the abbey church, looking down the ruined nave, with the galilee porch in the foreground

Facing page: The arcades of the east end, added to the original church in the early 13th century. The style of the new building was in marked contrast to the austerity of the earlier church

❶ GALILEE PORCH

The church is entered through the remains of a porch known as a galilee, a characteristic feature of Cistercian churches. Among other uses, it was a popular burial place for lay patrons until about 1300, and traces of eight graves remain. A tomb to the left of the central door carries the name of Isabel de Ros, who died in 1264; on the other side is a grave with a sloped covering bearing the inscription 'Hic iacet Jordanus' ('Here lies Jordan').

Above: A label stop from the refurbishment of the abbey in the 14th century
Right: The remains of the mosaic tiled floor in the nave

❷ NAVE

The church is cruciform (cross-shaped) in plan, with a nave – the main body of the church – transepts (side arms), and presbytery, or east end. Of the older parts of the church, the nave and its

narrow flanking aisles are the most ruined. The aisles served as corridors of access for the different functions of the nave. Contemporary with them are the lower west walls of the transepts (easily recognized by the same brown stone), which were

The 12th-century Church

The architecture of the original church mixed grandeur with simplicity. Raised on a terraced platform above the rest of the monastery, the church dominated every other building in the complex, and provided a place for daily devotion for the 600-strong community plus visitors. Design was simplified, with square ends adopted for the transepts, chapels and presbytery, and no tower over the crossing. Building materials were extremely plain, mainly rubble set in lime mortar plastered over and lime-washed inside and out, with the church thus standing white against the green hillside. Dressed stone was restricted to doorways, piers, arches and string-courses (horizontal mouldings on the surface of the walls). All these qualities – repeated, with some variation, at other Cistercian monasteries – made for a distinctive statement of reform. It contrasted sharply with the more ornamental architecture of the other monastic orders, such as the Benedictines in their cathedral churches.

Left: A reconstruction drawing of lay brothers worshipping in the western part of the church in the 12th century

heightened in the 1230s when a second clerestory or window level, with large windows, was added using a lighter stone. It is clear from this that the older church was about 5m (16ft) lower than the extension. The nave was supported by an arcade of pointed arches springing from square piers that rested on tall bases, angled about 1.5m (5ft) above the ground. A wooden barrel vault, described at the Suppression in 1538 as a painted ceiling, covered the nave. The aisles were also barrel vaulted in stone, with their vaults at right angles to that of the nave, in the manner of Cistercian churches in Burgundy. Architectural decoration was restricted to very simple mouldings. The ground plan, forms of vaulting, piers and unadorned wall surfaces were typical of the Cistercians' early churches. Melrose in Scotland, a daughter house of Rievaulx, may have been similar. The model for both churches was probably Clairvaux in Burgundy, from where the founder community at Rievaulx came.

When in use, the nave would not have been bare and undivided as it is now. It consists of nine

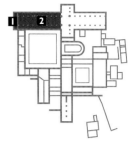

Above: The Cistercian abbey church of Fontenay in Burgundy. The style of vaulting, with the aisle vaults at right angles to that of the nave, was also used at Rievaulx

Left: The nave and transepts, seen from the north aisle of the nave. Note how the colour of the stone changes in the transept walls: this marks the 13th-century rebuilding of the east end

The Monastic Day

The day-to-day activities of the early medieval monks were governed by the rising and setting of the sun.

It is difficult to provide a precise timetable for a Cistercian monastic day, the daily *horarium*. Custom varied over the centuries and the arrangements altered with the seasons and between fasting days and others. As a guiding principle, all occupations of the monastic day were to be completed between the rising and the setting of the sun. The chart opposite gives only an indication of 'typical' days in the earlier medieval period.

Daily life consisted of three main parts, the first and most time-consuming of which was the *opus Dei* or church offices. Following the example of the Old Testament psalmist who praised God seven times a day and arose at midnight to give thanks (Psalm 119), the monks attended eight services or offices composed of psalms, the scriptures and prayer. There was also a daily Mass. The earliest office of Nocturns took place (in summer) at 2 a.m. and the last was Compline at 8 p.m.

The second part of the day was the *lectio divina* or spiritual reading, which lasted about two hours and took place in the cloister after the chapter meeting. At this meeting, held in the early morning, the monks discussed business and heard a chapter of the *Rule of St Benedict*.

Throughout the day, the monks were confined within the cloister (literally an enclosed space, from the Latin *claustrum*), except for the third part of the daily routine, the *opus manuum* or manual labour. Depending on the time of year, this lasted between two and four hours, and took place in the afternoon following the single main meal of the day, which was eaten in the refectory. Manual labour took several forms, determined by the skill, age and temperament of the individual monk. Gardening, agricultural work and joinery might be included, while the younger monks copied manuscripts. Where needed, buildings or workshops would be provided outside the cloister.

For the lay brothers, a different routine prevailed. They performed greater amounts of manual work than the monks, often at granges or outlying farms. For their two daily offices in church, the lay brothers used the western part of the nave.

Above: Cistercian monks in a choir, from a late 15th-century stained-glass window, originally from Altenburg Abbey in Germany but now in St Mary's Church, Shrewsbury

Below: Detail from a 12th-century Cistercian manuscript, showing a monk chopping down a tree

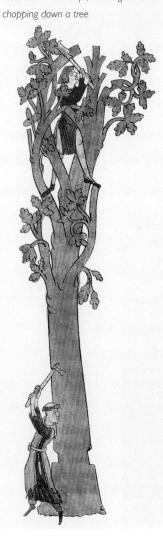

Summer	
1.30 a.m.	**Rise**
2 a.m.	**Nocturns** (later called Matins)
3.30 a.m.	**Matins** (Lauds) Rest – Reading
6 a.m.	**Prime** Chapter meeting Work
8 a.m.	**Terce** Mass Reading
11.30 a.m.	**Sext** Dinner Rest Work
2.30 p.m.	**None** Work Supper
6 p.m.	**Vespers** Collation reading
8 p.m.	**Compline**
8.15 p.m.	Retire to bed

Winter	
2.30 a.m.	**Rise**
3.30 a.m.	**Nocturns** (later Matins) Reading
6 a.m.	**Matins** (Lauds) **Prime** Reading
8 a.m.	**Terce** Mass Chapter meeting Work
noon	**Sext** Mass
1.30 p.m.	**None** Dinner Work
4.15 p.m.	**Vespers** Collation reading
6.15 p.m.	**Compline**
6.30 p.m.	Retire to bed

bays, or spaces between the piers. Starting from the west, bays two to five were occupied by the lay brothers' stalls, facing inwards against the low wall that divided the central area from the aisles. At the sixth bay, a rood screen across the nave – carrying an image of Christ on the cross and fronted by an altar – divided the west part of the church from that of the monks in the east parts. The next two bays – the retrochoir – were used by the old and infirm members of the community. Beyond, occupying the last bay of the nave and extending under the crossing (the space at the centre of the church, where the nave, presbytery and transepts meet), was the monks' choir, again with inward-facing stalls. The presbytery of the original church lay to the east and was a small, box-like space. It was probably lower in height than the transepts and nave, which meant that, as in many early Cistercian churches, there was no tower over the crossing. This allowed for a range of east-facing windows to light the choir at dawn and to mark the end of Matins, the first monastic office of the day. The aisles served as corridors for access between the parts of the church.

NAVE: LATER FEATURES

The older church and its interior divisions remained in place for nearly 100 years. By the early 14th century, however, the lay brothers had all but disappeared from Cistercian life, and as a consequence their choir stalls in the western parts of the nave were dismantled, leaving the nave free for processional use.

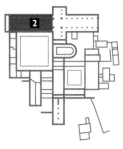

At the same time the nave was updated with new and larger windows containing tracery and stained glass. Although there were fewer monks, the proportion of priests among them was higher, and chapels were inserted into the eastern bays of the aisles, closest to the transepts, providing eight additional chapels in which the monks could say private Masses. Their altars and fittings survive in part; sockets for the screens are visible on the nave piers and side walls.

The remains of the early 15th-century tomb of Abbot Henry Burton (d.1429) can be seen in the eastern chapel on the south side. The doorway from the south aisle into the west alley of the cloister dates to the late 14th century. Beside the doorway into the east cloister alley is a fine piscina, or holy water basin, of similar date.

From the early 13th century onwards the floor of the church was paved with glazed tiles, forming various geometric designs and patterns. When the church was cleared in the early 1920s, many fragments of tiles were found and some were reset. Areas of tiling survive at the west end and other parts of the nave, and in the south transept. More complete areas of tiling were lifted and removed, some to the British Museum and some to the Doric Temple on the Rievaulx Terrace (see page 44).

Left: Detail of the piscina, or holy water basin, which dates from the late 14th-century remodelling of the nave

Below left: A priest celebrating Mass, from a 14th-century English Cistercian manuscript. At this date altars were inserted in the nave (and elsewhere) at Rievaulx to allow the monks to say private Masses

Below: This fragment of 15th-century painted glass, depicting a cockerel, was found during excavation of the church

Bottom: One of the decorated floor tiles from the nave, inscribed with the words '[Ave] Maria', c.1300

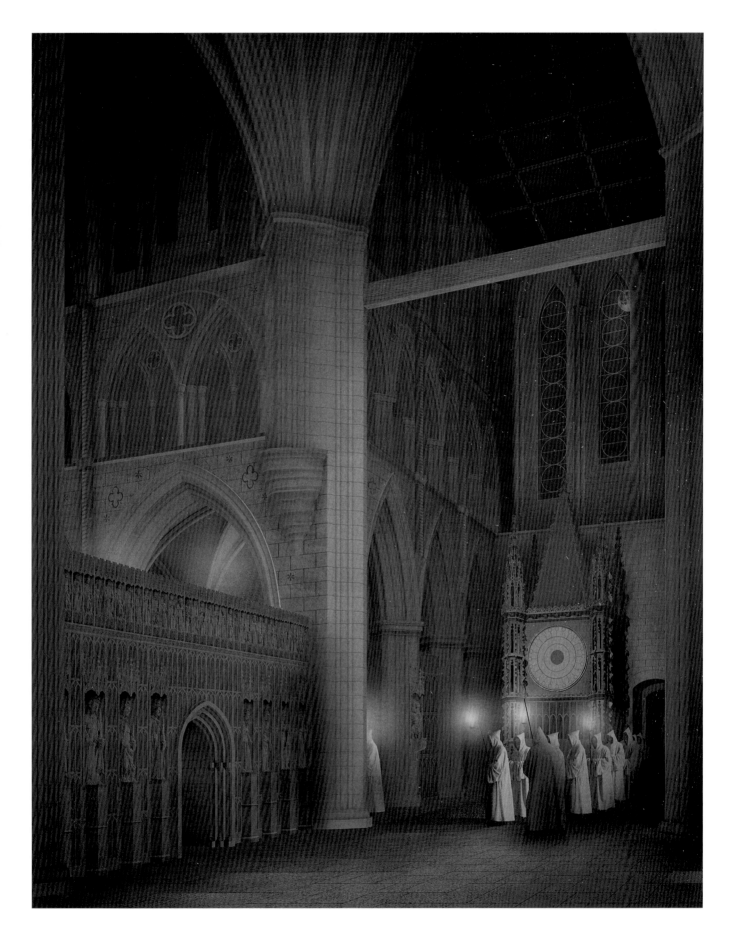

3 4 MONKS' CHOIR AND CROSSING

The monks' choir was in the two bays closest to the crossing, and the foundations for their stalls can still be seen in the grass. Many of the piers have holes and cuts (now visibly filled in) that indicate where fixtures such as screens, lamps or images would have been placed. In the eastern crossing piers, sockets show the location of the pulpitum or screen which separated the new choir from the nave, and the loft above it.

Nearby, close to the upper choir entrance in the south arcade, are the remains of a laver or basin where the monks performed a ritual washing before they entered the church; grooves in the stonework mark the housing for lead water pipes that fed it. Inventories made at the Suppression mention that a great timber press for vestments and a cupboard for service books once stood in the south aisle. These lay close to a sacristy – the room in which sacred vessels were stored – which was added to the south of the church in the 14th century.

A tower was raised over the vaulted crossing when the new east end was built; it contained a bell chamber and was topped with a timber steeple. At the Suppression, the floor of the south transept was covered with fallen timbers, lead and bells, suggesting that the steeple must have fallen some time before 1538.

5 6 NORTH AND SOUTH TRANSEPTS

In the original church, both transepts had three square-ended chapels in their east walls. When the church was extended, the side walls of the transepts were rebuilt to match the height of the new presbytery. Two new chapels were made in each transept, and the old inner chapels of the earlier church were cut through to make the aisles of the new church. A dramatic change in the colour and texture of the stone marks the junction between the old and new work. New windows were inserted in the heightened end (gable) walls, and a clerestory was added to the western side. In general the detailing is of poorer quality than in the presbytery and gives every impression of being hurried. The new transept chapels were vaulted to match the new presbytery aisles, but the transepts had a timber roof. Evidence of vault shafts in the inner bays indicates an intention to vault, and the decision to use timber must have been made during building.

Puzzlingly, the design of each transept differs. The north transept was built last: the clerestory windows here were a simplified version of those used in the presbytery. The most northerly chapel retains some of its stone rib vault. A new door was inserted in the gable wall to provide access to the monks' burial ground that lay to the north and east of the new building.

The south transept, which was built first, has details in the arcade and middle storey similar to those in the presbytery. Its gable wall had doors to the vestry (to the east) and to the dormitory for the night office (in the south-west corner). A fragment of the mosaic tiling which once covered the floor of the new building survives in front of the sacristy door, similar to the tiling that survives in the nave. The monks used the doorway from the dormitory here to enter the church for the first office at 2 a.m. or 3.30 a.m. every day (depending on the season). Close to the entry was a 15th-century clock in an elaborate wooden case (noted in the inventory compiled at the Suppression). A slot in the northern pier of the arcade held a bracket for a statue of St Christopher, placed where it could be seen by the monks as they entered the church. Viewing an image of St Christopher was believed to provide protection against dying that day without receiving the last sacrament and also against the tiredness resulting from daily toil.

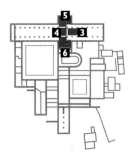

Above: Tiles just by the entrance to the north transept
Left: A view of the south transept today

Facing page: A reconstruction of the south transept in the 15th century, showing the monks processing from the night stairs towards the choir

7 PRESBYTERY

The eastern parts of the monks' church, or presbytery, can best be appreciated from the far end. This extension was rebuilt in the 1220s in a strikingly different style from the earlier nave. Much more detailed than that of the earlier church, the new architecture is marked by an increase in height with a three-storey elevation, numerous lancet windows and the daring rib vaulting of the main span. Piers, arcades, upper storeys and vaulting ribs are adorned throughout with thin and beautifully multiplied detailing, which dresses the supports and openings with a repeated finely scaled linearism composed of slim projecting forms and shadowed hollows. This elaboration was a far cry from the nave's blunt, unornamented bareness. The contrast is perhaps best explained by the monks' desire to celebrate the shrine of their third abbot, St Aelred (abbot 1147–67), with the most fitting and fashionable shrine architecture (see page 12).

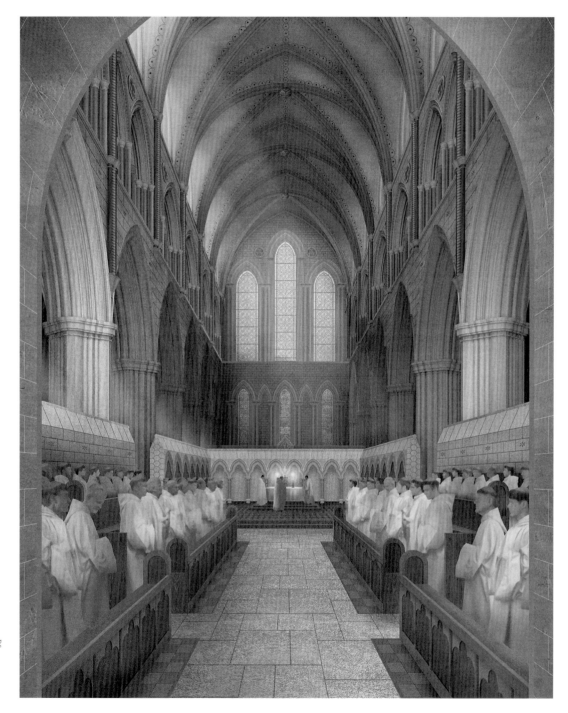

Above: A late medieval stone cross from the west end of the abbey church

Right: A reconstruction showing how the east end of the church may have looked after the 13th-century rebuilding

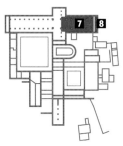

Left: The exterior of the east end of the church. Its seven-bay extension made the church one of the longest in the north of England
Below: Diagram showing the liturgical arrangement of the presbytery

The seven-bay extension made the Rievaulx church one of the longest in the north of England. Although a skeleton today, it consisted of four distinct parts. Next to the crossing, bays one and two served as the monks' choir; bays three, four and five contained the sanctuary with the high altar raised at the east end and St Aelred's shrine elevated behind it; bay six provided the ambulatory for circulation and the use of monks and pilgrims; and bay seven screened the five altars set against the terminal east wall.

The sequence of building went from east to west and may be followed in the fabric. Building began outside the old church, leaving its east end undisturbed for as long as possible. Only when work was far advanced towards the old church did the masons dismantle the earlier termination. Accurate siting of the new with the old work was therefore done blind. In fact, the new presbytery was built too close to the old church resulting in the bay next to the crossing being narrower than the other six bays and requiring the contraction of the arcade, middle storey and clerestory.

8 CHAPELS

Along the wall at the far east end are the altar bases and separating screens of five chapels, which provided for the more frequent private Masses common in the 13th century (and correspond to the higher proportion of priests among the monks at this time). We know from inventories made after the Suppression of Rievaulx in 1538 that the three central chapels contained images of St John the Baptist, St John the Evangelist and the Virgin Mary. The large lancet windows in the east wall allowed light to pour into this part of the church.

1 Chapels
2 Shrine of St Aelred
3 High altar
4 Choir

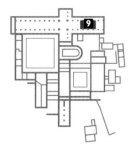

9

Right: View of the presbytery and high altar

Below right: Illustration of supplicants kneeling by an altar in front of a shrine, from a 15th-century French manuscript. People would have prayed in front of Aelred's shrine at Rievaulx

Right: The east end of the church

1 *The clerestory takes the form of paired lancet windows fronted by a single large opening, with an interior passage*

2 *The bays are divided by triple shafts rising from the base of the middle storey to provide support for the masonry vaults. The arcade arches are elegantly and intricately moulded*

3 *The middle storey is composed of pairs of large arches (once subdivided in two) and supported by multiple shafts, originally of Frosterley marble from Weardale, County Durham*

4 *Piers were composed of many clustered shafts, which rest on highly decorated bases*

9 SHRINE AND SANCTUARY

To the east of the choir, the sanctuary occupied the third, fourth and fifth bays of the new building and was framed by an arcaded stone screen. The floor was raised by two steps in the third bay and again by a single step in the fifth bay. Dominating the fifth bay was the high altar capped by a huge stone slab; overturned 500 years ago at the Suppression, it was recently raised from the ground and placed on a new base. The sixth bay served as an ambulatory or walkway; a doorway in the south wall provided access to the church for sick monks capable of walking the few feet from the infirmary lying to the south. This bay housed the gold and silver shrine containing the remains of St Aelred set above the arcaded stone screen. At the Suppression Henry VIII appropriated the shrine and melted it down. All that remains of this sacred area is a moulded bench-seat set just east of the high altar, which was used by the monks and pilgrims observing the medieval practice of 'watching', vigils associated with the holy of holies. The seventh bay accommodated the five altars set against the east wall, whose bases remain.

From the late 14th century, patrons of Rievaulx were buried between the piers outside the screen

framing the sanctuary. The base of the double grave of John de Ros (d.1393) and his wife, who died the following year, can be seen to the south of the high altar. Thomas de Ros, lord of Helmsley and patron of the abbey, was buried at the centre of the choir in 1384. Many fragments of tomb effigies were found when the eastern arm of the church was excavated in 1919, and it is likely that both the aisles and the area in front of the sanctuary were carpeted with graves.

Aelred: Abbot and Saint (1110–67)

Aelred's rule was marked by inclusivity and tolerance.

Aelred is the best known figure associated with Rievaulx. During his charismatic rule as abbot between 1147 and 1167, the monastery was renowned as a spiritual centre and attracted many gifts of land. Under Aelred, the abbey founded seven satellite monasteries in northern England and southern Scotland and doubled in size to over 600 men (140 monks, 500 lay brothers and laymen). Aelred also oversaw the construction of new buildings (see plan, inside back cover). A valued advisor of the new Angevin ruler of England, Henry II (r.1154–89), Aelred was also in demand as a conciliator, historian and biblical expositor.

Born in 1110 in Hexham into a family of high ecclesiastical standing, Aelred was schooled at Durham and trained for diplomacy at the court of David I of Scotland. Tall and handsome, he was entrusted with embassies to northern England in his early twenties. Contact with the Cistercians, however, and the attraction of Rievaulx led him to forsake court life for the austerity of a monastic novice. His 1142 *Speculum Caritatis* (Mirror of Charity), in which he developed the idea of the human person as an image of God, established him as a major spiritual writer. Similarly notable among his 20 books was a work from his late years, *De Spirituali Amicitia* (On Spiritual Friendship). Aelred had a deep devotion to northern Anglo-Saxon saints and was the author of a work on the saints of Hexham.

Much is also known of Aelred through the *Vita* authored by Walter Daniel, his friend and the abbey's infirmary master. Rich in personal detail, it characterizes Aelred's often unconventional but appealing model of authority. Renowned for his inclusivity and tolerance, qualities all the more remarkable in a monastic order better known for its exclusivity and strictness, Aelred drew many men across the North York moors to Rievaulx.

For his spiritual depth, pastoral insight, commitment to unity and written legacy, Aelred was raised to a saint in 1250. At about this time his relics (or remains) were moved to a shrine in the church. This was seen in the 1530s by John Leland, the Tudor antiquary. He described it as being of gold and silver, and this is likely to be the gilded shrine 'over' the high altar mentioned in the Suppression-era inventory. Leland also noted the presence of several of Aelred's works in the library at Rievaulx.

In 1476, the Cistercian General Chapter granted formal permission for the observation of Aelred's feast at Rievaulx, citing 'old and new miracles' in the church there. The feast was of high status and observed on the date of Aelred's death, 12 January; it is still celebrated on this date in the Catholic and Anglican Churches.

A life (or legend) of Aelred was written in the mid 15th century by the hagiographer John Capgrave (1393–1464). This was printed in 1516 together with the lives of other English saints. Aelred's name also occurs in the list of Cistercian saints printed in 1491 by the abbot of Cîteaux.

The saint's shrine at Rievaulx was a focus of devotion. In 1526 one John Rogerson bequeathed 'to Sancte Alred's shryne a paire of beades'. The abbey also had a 'girdle' of St Aelred, which was loaned to women to ease their pains during childbirth.

Below: Portrait of Aelred (kneeling), from a 14th-century manuscript of his Life of Edward the Confessor

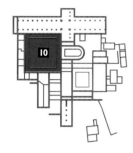

'The day before
yesterday, when I
was going round the
cloister of the
monastery, sitting
with the brethren in a
loving circle, as though
amid the delights of
paradise, I admired the
leaves, the flowers,
and the fruits of each
single tree.'
Aelred, De Spirituali
Amicitia, *mid 1160s*

Above: Aelred, abbot
of Rievaulx, from an
illuminated 13th-century
Cistercian manuscript
Right: The reconstructed
section of arcade
in the north-west corner
of the cloister

THE MONASTIC LAYOUT

At the centre of Rievaulx lay the church and the cloister with its surrounding buildings. Both followed reasonably standard plans. They were shared by the monks and lay brothers and were shaped by the different routines and duties of each group. The monks used the east parts of the church, the two-storey range of buildings that bordered the east side of the cloister and the single-storey range on the south. They were confined to the church and cloister for about 20 hours of each day. The lay brothers occupied the west parts of the church and the two-storey western range of the cloister. They only used the church, range and the cloister for about nine hours each day because of their work in the fields and on the granges. Their use of the cloister remains uncertain but the evidence of original doors and openings indicates that they had access to it – part of the inclusive character of the Cistercians into the 1170s.

10 THE CLOISTER

The area next to the south aisle of the church is the cloister. About 42m (140ft) square, it is one of the largest built by the Cistercians in Britain. Formed from another man-made platform about 1.5m (5ft) lower than the church, the cloister was an open square or garth laid out as a garden and perhaps planted with fruit trees at the centre. It was originally surrounded by a roofed arcade, carried on a seat-high stylobate, or supporting platform, by paired shafts with foliate capitals which support plain arches, some of which have been re-erected in the north-west corner from debris found during the 1920s clearance. The first, small church raised in the 1130s lies underneath the north-east quadrant of the cloister, before the community replaced it in about 1150 with the larger church described above.

The monks used the north alley beside the church for reading and study – the daily *lectio divina* or spiritual reading, lasting for two hours – and the Suppression documents mention the monks' carrels or desks. The north alley was also where the monks gathered immediately before bed to hear a reading from the *Collations* of St John Cassian, a fourth-century writer on monastic life.

In the exterior (west) wall of the transept is a large arched recess for a cupboard in which the monks kept the books being used in the cloister. Next to it is the entrance to the main abbey library. Immediately beyond is a shallow rectangular recess in the wall which held a wax tablet on which the roster for the monks' weekly duties was kept.

The cloister had alleys on each side, which were supported by round-headed arches on elegant twin shafts. Another door to the church in the north-west corner of the cloister was used by the monks for their Sunday processions.

The Library at Rievaulx

The library at Rievaulx once contained over 200 books – the majority on theological subjects – of which 22 survive.

In obedience to Chapter 48 of the *Rule of St Benedict*, choir monks spent a portion of each day reading in the cloister. The books used in the cloister, the church, infirmary and refectory, were stored in a cupboard (*armarium*) in the large round-headed recess which can be seen next to the entrance to the church in the east aisle of the cloister.

There was also a library at Rievaulx, which was reached through the first doorway on the east side of the cloister. The library contained 225 books, described in two catalogues dating to the late 12th or early 13th century. These were divided into 16 categories or classes, labelled from A (legal texts, including works by the 12th-century jurist Gratian and Justinian's *Digest* of Roman law) to Q (a miscellaneous group with no obvious rationale). The majority of books were on theological subjects, but there were also historical works by authors such as Bede, Henry of Huntingdon and Eusebius, and a small number of works by classical authors, such as Cicero and philosophers, including Boethius. The psalters of former abbots were also preserved in the library.

Cistercian writers, especially Bernard of Clairvaux, feature prominently in the catalogues. Many of the books were by abbots and monks of Rievaulx. The first catalogue lists 14 works by Aelred and eight by Maurice. John Leland, antiquary of Henry VIII, made a brief description of the library shortly before the abbey was closed down in 1538. He focused on local authors, recording several works by Aelred and nine by his biographer, Walter Daniel.

Only 22 books survive from the monastery's once substantial library. They are now in the collections of libraries in the United Kingdom, Ireland and France. Most can be identified by the ownership, or *ex libris*, inscription, *Liber Sancte Marie Rievallis*, 'Book of St Mary of Rievaulx'. Seven of these surviving books can be linked with volumes listed in the medieval catalogues.

Above: Medieval book fittings, found at Rievaulx

Below left: John Stell, a Cistercian scribe from Furness Abbey, writing a verse on a scroll, from the Cartulary of Furness Abbey, 1412

Below: Detail of the 12th-century manuscript Rabanus super Matheum, *inscribed with the words* Liber Sancte Marie Rievallis, *indicating that it was originally from Rievaulx*

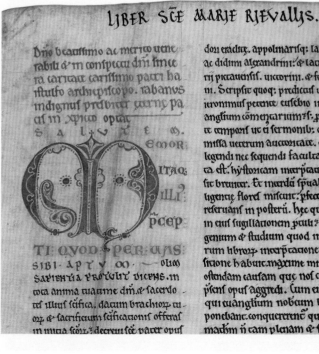

Above: Cistercian lay brothers occupied the west range of the cloister. They can be distinguished from the choir monks by their brown robes and beards, as shown in this early 12th-century manuscript illustration of a lay brother reaping corn

Below: The west range

1 *Original parlour, later the site of the lay brothers' night stair*

2 *Stone base for wooden post to support the dormitory above*

3 *Later parlour*

4 *Lay brothers' refectory*

▐ WEST RANGE

The two-storeyed west range of a Cistercian monastery housed the lay brothers. The ground floor served as their refectory and parlour and also provided cellarage for the monastery's kitchen. The entire first floor was occupied by their dormitory, with a night stair descending into the western part of the church nave. It was not unusual for their buildings to be among the earliest in a monastery as the lay brothers did much of the construction work. This is the case at Rievaulx and the west range contains the earliest Cistercian architecture not only in England but even on the Continent. When first built, it would have been home to about 125 lay brothers. Although much ruined, it is important because it is all that survives from the time of the first and founder abbot, William (abbot 1132–45). Narrow and unvaulted, the range has minimal architectural detail – a hallmark of the austerity of early Cistercian architecture.

The best view of the west range is from the steps beside the doorway to the nave. This area was the parlour, where members of the community might meet with family on limited occasions. At the far end, beyond eight bays of cellars, was the refectory or dining hall; its broad servery arch now leads into the cloister alley, but originally opened into the kitchen of the earliest south range. The wooden floor of the dormitory above was supported on substantial wooden posts which stood on a central row of stone bases, some of which survive. A latrine for the dormitory would have projected westwards from the main range – a low arch in the west wall of the lay brothers' refectory may mark the position of the latrine drain where it passes under the west range. On the outer west wall, cuts for a lean-to roof show that there was a covered alley there.

The range was remodelled several times in the abbey's 400-year history to adjust to changes in use. In about 1190 the entrance passage was remodelled and rib vaults inserted to provide a grander parlour; the old parlour became the site of an enlarged night stair from the dormitory into the church. Such changes were clearly made with an eye to the semi-public function of this part of the range. At about the same time new doorways were inserted in the east and west walls, and a porch was built outside the new parlour door with a lodging beyond and over it, recorded as the 'chambers over the parlour door' in inventories made at the Suppression.

From about 1300, after the lay brothers had ceased to be part of the community, the range was extensively remodelled. Partition walls were inserted in the northern half of the range, providing private studies or offices for the senior monks or abbey officials. At the same time the former dormitory on the upper floor became a granary, to store grain for the brewhouse and bakehouse that lay to the west in the inner court. The southern end of the range was demolished and a new end wall constructed.

SOUTH RANGE

The buildings on the south side of the cloister include the kitchen, refectory (dining hall) and warming house. The refectory is set at right angles to the cloister, in a layout peculiar to Cistercian abbeys, which was initially adopted in the 1160s. Before that the Cistercians had used the standard Benedictine arrangement with the refectory set parallel to the south cloister alley. The first refectory at Rievaulx followed this plan and occupied the southern part of the present cloister, but the third abbot, Aelred, demolished it, added its area to the cloister court, and built a new refectory further south, possibly to the new Cistercian plan. This range in turn was largely demolished and replaced in the late 12th century by the present buildings.

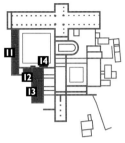

12 Kitchen

The first doorway on the right leads into the kitchen. This room is badly ruined, but some details of its layout survive. When first built it had a row of arches on the south side with an aisle beyond and was covered with ribbed vaults. There was probably a central fireplace with a large chimney stack. The ragged hole in the east wall is the food hatch through to the refectory. Part of its curved side remains, showing that it held a rotating shelf, or dumb waiter, which could be locked in the closed position. On its left-hand side is a recess for a cupboard.

The kitchen was extensively remodelled in the 15th century, when the south wall and the vaulting were taken down, and a new south wall with a large fireplace was built. A flagged and kerbed washing area can still be seen in the floor opposite.

13 Refectory Undercroft

A modern timber staircase leads down through a doorway into the refectory cellar or undercroft. This large room was vaulted with a central row of piers, though scars on the south wall and a blocked central window show that it was originally intended to have two rows of piers. The piers were encased with additional stonework to reinforce them, but this does not seem to have been wholly effective, for many show signs of failure. Several cross walls divide the undercroft, and include parts of windows and doorways, indicating that they were built from reused stone. There is a flagged washing area with kerbed edges at the south, larger than that in the kitchen and suggesting that the undercroft served as a laundry area at some time.

Following the Suppression the undercroft (or perhaps the refectory above) served as a charcoal store, supplying fuel to the nearby blast furnace producing iron – a change of use that ensured its survival (see page 42).

14 Laver

The monks entered their refectory through a large, richly moulded doorway in the south cloister alley, which is flanked by wide recesses filled with arcading and featuring trefoil-headed arches. These recesses represent the monks' laver, where they washed before meals. Lead pipes provided a water supply to a series of taps set below the arcading, and discharged into a long trough described at the Suppression as being of 'lead overcast with pewter'. A series of sockets above the laver arcading marks the position of the cloister roof.

As well as being used for everyday washing, the wall-mounted laver served as a place of ritual. On Saturdays it was used for the ceremonial washing of the monks' feet by the abbot, in emulation of Christ's washing of the Disciples' feet before the Last Supper when he enjoined them to follow a new commandment, or mandate, to love one another. This important weekly commemoration, the *mandatum*, was raised to sacramental status by Bernard of Clairvaux. At Rievaulx, the monks sat on a raised bench above the laver, the end of which may be seen on the east side, and placed their feet in the washing trough.

Above: Christ washing the feet of the Disciples, from a 13th-century French manuscript. This act, or mandatum, *was commemorated at Rievaulx every Saturday at the laver trough*

Below: Flanking the refectory entrance was the laver, where the monks washed before meals in a pewter-lined trough under the wall arcades

13 Refectory

The refectory hall is best viewed through the doorway from the cloister. This large, light-filled room is the finest monastic refectory in Britain.

The refectory floor was at cloister level and had fixed tables supported on stone legs that were set into the floor. The tables were arranged around the side walls, and at the end there would have been a dais or raised platform forming a high table for the prior and senior monks. The monks ate their meals in strict silence while listening to the day's reading, which was delivered by one of the monks from the pulpit. This was contained within a large recess, now ruined, in the west wall of the room and was reached via a staircase. Fragments recovered during excavation show that the pulpit had an arcaded balustrade, with Frosterley marble shafts supporting a sloping bookrest.

Around the upper walls, the windows are set in an ornate arcade. Above them are clusters of small triple shafts in the upper side walls which supported the original roof, probably a barrel ceiling, while the large corbels with vertical grooves above them carried the later, 15th-century roof. The far south wall has three lancet windows in the gable which were reduced in height to accord with the form of the roof.

Above: A reconstruction of the refectory as it may have looked in about 1500. Readings were given from the pulpit (on the right) while the monks ate in silence. The painted decoration can be reconstructed from traces of paint that survive on the masonry

Far right: A scene in a monastic refectory, showing St Benedict finding flour and feeding the monks, part of a 15th-century fresco cycle by Luca Signorelli and Giovanni Sodoma in the abbey of Monte Oliveto Maggiore, Italy

Right: An early 16th-century Cistercian-ware cup from Rievaulx Abbey

Food and Drink in the Monastery

The Cistercians took meals twice a day in summer and once in winter. The principal, and first, meal occurred in the late morning – about 11.30am in summer (later in winter). In the summer a second, lighter meal was eaten in the late afternoon.

Monastic diet varied with the seasons, depending on the

vegetables and fruits (all grown by the community) that were available. The *Rule of St Benedict* ordained a vegetarian diet for all except the sick, who were allowed to eat meat. Bread and beans were staples, washed down with ale (brewed without hops). The main hot food consisted of potage, a thick, porridge-like soup sometimes enriched with milk and cheese and in the later Middle Ages with eggs. The monks also occasionally ate fish and eels.

By the 1340s a gradual drift towards the consumption of meat had begun. It was eaten once or twice a week but had

to be cooked in a separate kitchen and eaten in a separate refectory, probably located in the abbot's hall.

The warming house has a complex building history, and was remodelled several times, initially while Aelred was abbot. Much of what is now visible dates to a rebuilding of the late 12th century. At this date, it was a single-storey building, with three round-headed windows in the north (cloister) wall. It had an elegant arcade standing on tall octagonal piers with an aisle on the far (south) side. In the west wall was a pair of large hearths divided by a slender central shaft.

The building was altered again shortly afterwards, when a room was created above it. A stone vault was inserted, carried on two piers of the arcade, which were heavily reinforced to support the vault. Later still, when the number of monks was much reduced, the aisle was removed and the arcade walled up. The upper room may have been 'the house for evidence' mentioned at the Suppression and could have served to store the abbey's valuable charters and documents.

At the east end of the room there is a stone sink, with a hole for a lead pipe and a flagged floor in front of it with kerbed edging. This was where the monks washed their laundry in the winter and hung their clothes to dry before the fire (which may explain the need for the double fireplace). There is more flagging and kerbing for another washing area in the defunct aisle.

Traces of paint round the arch heads show that the room was painted pale pink with a fine false masonry pattern. Around the head of the entrance doorway there was a fish-scale pattern of overlapping semicircles. The mouldings of the wall arcades were also painted red. The interior would have been remarkably light, with its 27 windows, and richly decorated with continuous arcading and carved capitals. As such it stood in stark contrast to the simplicity of the church, built 20 years earlier, and reflects the changes in architecture in the last quarter of the 12th century when early Gothic forms were replacing the Romanesque.

15 Warming House

To the left of the refectory is the warming house, entered through a plain doorway in the south-east corner of the cloister. A fire was lit here on All Saints' Day (1 November) and kept burning throughout the winter months until Good Friday so that the monks might warm themselves.

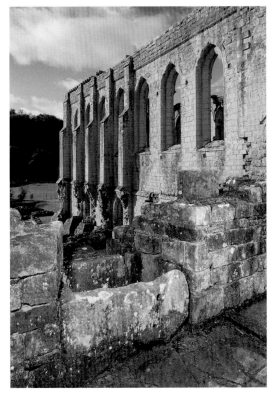

Above left: The refectory and its undercroft, seen through the doorway from the cloister
Above: A 15th-century foliate corbel from the later refectory roof
Left: The stone sink in the warming house. The monks washed their laundry here

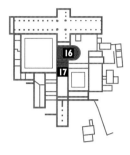

Below: This plaited metal scourge, used to administer punishment or for self-penance, was found during clearance of the abbey in 1924

Below right: A reconstruction of the chapter house in the 14th century, seen from the same angle as the photograph opposite. By this time the building had been reduced in size by removing the aisles, and traceried windows had been inserted

EAST RANGE

16 Chapter House

After the church, the chapter house was the most important building in the monastery. Here the daily chapter meetings were held, at which the monks heard a reading of a chapter from the *Rule of St Benedict* (hence the name given to the building), commemorated their deceased brethren, discussed secular business matters, confessed their faults and received punishment. Depending on the misdemeanour, this ranged from reducing their food to bread and water to flogging and even imprisonment. The room was also the place where distinguished guests were received, sermons were delivered by the abbot, monks and lay brothers took their solemn vows as full members of the community and abbots were buried.

The chapter house at Rievaulx is of unusual design. It extends well east of the range and terminated with a rounded end. The interior resembled a church with a central high space flanked by lower aisles. The main space was supported by an arcade carried on columns and surmounted by a wooden barrel vault, and the surrounding aisle was rib vaulted. Tiered stone benches lined the length of the main space and the aisles were also benched along their length. Seating was therefore provided for most of the community including the lay brothers. Among the occasions when they joined the monks were the 12 major feast days, when sermons were preached by the abbot speaking in the vernacular so that they could be understood by the lay brothers; those who could not fit into the chapter house stood in the cloister and heard his words through three large openings and the doorways.

Following the reduction in the numbers of monks, in the 14th century the eastern arcades were walled up and the aisle partly taken down. At the Suppression the building was demolished; the piers in the south arcade bear chisel marks where they were broken. This process was not without danger, for the skeletons of two of the demolition gang were discovered during 20th-century excavation of the room; presumably they were killed during an unexpected collapse.

The chapter house was entered from the cloister by three doorways. The central one is of elaborate design and was flanked by unglazed two-light openings with round-headed arches. The opening nearest to the church was later filled with a remarkable shrine dating from 1250. It commemorates the first abbot, William (d.1145), whose burial casket would have stood on the upper shelf; the lower shelf allowed pilgrims to crawl inside to be closer to the saint.

In the cloister alley in front of the shrine is a metal grille, beneath which can be seen part of the cloister wall of Abbot William's first east range.

17 Parlour and Treasury

The plain doorway to the south of the chapter house leads into a long narrow room which was used as the parlour. Here essential conversation could be conducted briefly without breaking the rule of silence enforced throughout the cloister.

The corbels on the side walls supported a ribbed vault, and there are stone benches along both sides.

In the south wall is a doorway into a narrow room with a vaulted ceiling that is thought to have served as a treasury. Here valuables belonging to the abbey and local landowners could be safely stored in the small cupboards or niches set into its side walls. In the east wall an original window has been altered at its base to create a doorway; when this was made, the entrance from the parlour was probably walled up.

Left: The chapter house, where the monks' daily chapter meeting was held, is the most remarkable of the buildings dating from Aelred's time
Above: Two gold nobles found in the treasury at Rievaulx
Below: The parlour – the only room in the cloister in which monks were allowed to speak

18 19 Day Stairs and Passage

Just by the entrance to the parlour in the cloister is a flight of steps projecting into the cloister alley. This was the day stair, which would have risen in a straight flight to the dormitory. It was used by the monks during the day, when they had the option of a short siesta. Only the lower side posts of the doorway remain.

The next doorway beyond the day stairs gave access to a passage through the east range to the infirmary cloister (see page 25). The passage was covered by a barrel vault. A doorway in its south wall leads to some steps down into a large space which was known as the day room.

The east range once continued another 30m (100ft) beyond the south wall of the latrine, where because of the terracing of the site it was three storeys high. This end of the range suffered badly from subsidence and had to be propped up with huge flying buttresses. Eventually the monks abandoned it as living space: it was unroofed, reduced in height, and the ground floor was used for tanning leather – the tanning vats, built from roof tiles, still survive (see page 27).

21 Novices' Room and Latrine Block

In the south-east corner of the day room is a door that led at ground level to a room for teaching the novices – those admitted for a probationary period of training before taking their full profession as monks. This stood over a barrel-vaulted cellar, and was covered by a second barrel vault supporting another floor above. On this first floor was the main reredorter, or latrine, of the monastery, which had a row of lavatory seats set over the main abbey drain. A pair of doorways, one for entry and one for exit, can still be seen high up in the east wall of the dormitory above. The eastern end of the latrine block was later remodelled and reduced in length; another block once projected south at its eastern end, but this has been completely demolished.

20 Day Room and Dormitory

The day room was divided down the centre by a row of piers supporting groin vaulting, formed by intersecting barrel vaults. Simple squared ribs defined each vault compartment. There are fireplaces in both side walls. In winter the monks retreated from the cloister into this room to work. The younger monks would copy manuscripts and read, while the older monks engaged in light crafts such as sewing and mending garments. At the south end of the room was a latrine, set over the main abbey drain, which was flushed with running water.

The whole of the first floor of the east range originally formed the monks' dormitory. This was a huge room about 73m (240ft) long in which the monks slept on mattresses. Under Aelred their numbers rose to 140, but even such a large room would have seemed crowded with so many sleeping in it. However, its end (south) wall was rebuilt in the 15th century when the east range was drastically reduced in length. Enlarged twin-light windows were created at this time and no doubt the room was divided up with partitions into individual rooms or cells. This reflected not only a decline in the number of monks but also a rising standard of comfort and an increasing expectation of privacy.

Above left: A sculpture of a Cistercian monk reading, from Eberbach Abbey, Germany, c.1375. Monks at Rievaulx would have read in the day room
Above: Detail of the tiled floor in the day room
Left: The basement of the latrine block. The novices' room was at ground-floor level above this, with the latrine on the first floor above

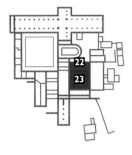

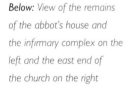

INFIRMARY COMPLEX

On the east side of the monks' dormitory was the infirmary, which provided for the sick and the older members of the community. All of these buildings were constructed under Abbot Aelred in the late 1150s. They form the earliest surviving infirmary complex on any Cistercian site in Britain. Three hundred years later, the original buildings were greatly modified by their conversion in the 1490s into a monumental house for Abbot John Burton.

Subsequent demolition has made both the infirmary and later abbot's house difficult to understand. The plan of the latter, however, can be recovered from inventory descriptions written in the late 1530s, while the layout of the infirmary can be determined by studying the remains.

Below: View of the remains of the abbot's house and the infirmary complex on the left and the east end of the church on the right

22 Early Abbot's House (Long House)

The north side of the infirmary cloister was formed by the abbot's house, custom-built for Aelred with a dispensation from the General Chapter of the Cistercian Order when illness made it impossible for him to sleep in the common dormitory, the usual practice for Cistercian abbots. It may be reached by a short flight of steps. Only the ground floor of Aelred's house survives. The central square room was originally vaulted; a larger room that lay to the west was probably his hall, two storeys high. The abbot's chamber would have been on the first floor above the smaller room.

It was here, according to Aelred's biographer Walter Daniel, the infirmary master, that Aelred wrote the literary and spiritual treatises that earned him an international reputation. An impressive porch was built in the 1160s between the abbot's house, which was closed by a door, and the chapter house. A bench for those awaiting entry still survives opposite the door.

In the 13th century five new double windows – of which only the bases remain – were inserted into the north wall; these are now only visible from the exterior. A door was cut through into the treasury at this time.

The abbot's house continued in use until about 1490. After that, the buildings were much altered: among other changes, the first floor was extended across the north alley of the infirmary cloister, providing a first-floor gallery for the abbot's use which became known as the 'long house'.

23 Infirmary Cloister

The infirmary was served by its own smaller cloister for the use of the sick and elderly monks. The cloister was surrounded on all four sides with an open arcade, a section of which has been reconstructed to show its original form: the capitals are generally simpler in design than those of the main cloister.

The enclosed garth was almost certainly a garden (in 1537–8 it was called the Abbot's Garden) used for growing the herbs that were central to medieval medicine. In the 15th century the western and southern alleys of the infirmary cloister were removed and the arcades of the northern and part of the eastern alley were partially blocked, as part of the conversion of the infirmary into the abbot's house.

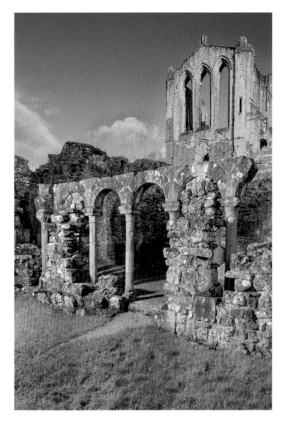

Left: Part of the arcade of the infirmary cloister, reconstructed in its north-west corner
Below: An early 14th-century illustration of blood-letting. The Cistercians underwent blood-letting four times a year (unlike the Benedictines, who did it six times). Regular blood-letting was thought to remove bodily impurities, correct imbalance of the humours and reduce sexual appetite
Below left: A monk lying ill in bed, with an abbot and two monks beside him, from a 13th-century French manuscript

Sickness and Health

At a great monastery such as Rievaulx, monks as well as lay people from the surrounding area could receive medical help. Monk-physicians treated the sick and made visits outside the abbey, although officially the Cistercians discouraged such contacts. Monasteries also nurtured the study of medicine, keeping collections of case histories, libraries of medical manuscripts and supporting staff who specialized in medical work.

Within the monastery the sick and their carers were closely integrated with the community. The sick at Rievaulx were tended in three separate infirmary buildings: east of the main cloister for the monks, in the inner court for the lay brothers and servants, and just outside the great gatehouse for visitors, travellers or those in the immediate vicinity. Only the monks' infirmary survives.

The huge size of the infirmary hall – as large as the nave of the church – together with its generous lighting and provision of fireplaces, highlights the emphasis given to health and care within the monastery. Apart from the sick and elderly, the infirmary also served short-stay patients. Its scale may also relate to the medieval belief that illness was the result of corrupted air, and to the desire to ennoble the carers as well as the patients.

Medieval medicine was based on pharmacological rather than invasive means and relied on herbal preparations. Its effectiveness was helped by

general hygiene and the better diet permitted in the infirmary. Simple surgical procedures were also undertaken, including blood-letting, which was an accepted part of medieval medicine. Since significant amounts of blood were drawn, the monks were allowed to recuperate in the infirmary.

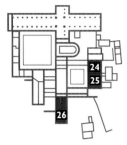

24 Infirmary

From the infirmary cloister, the round-headed door on the far (east) side leads into the infirmary itself. This was first built when the community was approaching 140 monks, and comprised a great hall of 12 bays, running north to south, with a single aisle on its eastern side.

It was a vast space, almost as big as the nave of the church, and retains enough detail to show how it functioned. Seven of the squat piers of the eastern arcade survive – two have been reconstructed and their capitals reset. Sockets in some of the piers show that the building was divided by timber partitions into a series of smaller rooms in which the beds for the sick monks were placed. There is an original fireplace in the east wall.

Early in the 13th century a door and stair were inserted into the north wall of the infirmary to allow the monks to attend services in the church via a covered gallery. Later, privacy within the infirmary hall was increased when the timber screens were replaced by stone walls and the arcade arches were also blocked with stone walls, so providing individual cubicles for the monks.

By the later 14th century these rooms had been reordered to provide two-roomed apartments. The infirmary kitchen, which can still be identified despite later remodelling, lay east of the hall. To the north-east of that was a substantial early

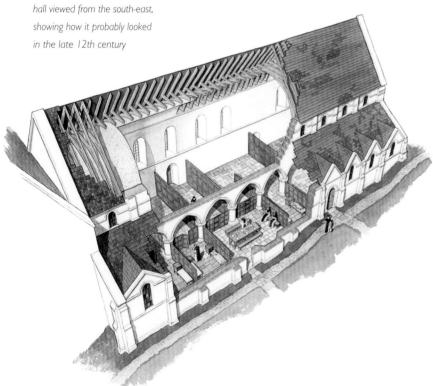

13th-century building that probably housed the infirmarer. In the south wall of the infirmary a door on the line of the arcade led into the infirmary latrine and the bathhouse beyond it. Warm baths were considered an important part of cures.

25 Later Abbot's House

The great infirmary was much too large for the late medieval community at Rievaulx. In the late 15th century it was taken over by Abbot John Burton, who remodelled it to create a remarkable new house that marked his, and the abbey's, social status.

The central part of the infirmary became the abbot's hall at first-floor level: the great rectangular block of masonry in the middle of the infirmary was inserted to carry a central hearth. A fine new door was inserted in the west wall, reached by stairs from the old infirmary cloister.

To the north of the hall, John Burton added a two-storey cross-wing with a bay window to the east. The ground floor here was the abbot's parlour with a fireplace in its north wall, while the upper floor was his great chamber – a private living room where he would meet important visitors. Pinholes in the surviving walls show that both the parlour and great chamber would have been panelled. At the south end of the old infirmary were two or more chambers, one with a latrine, which were probably used by important visitors.

The ground floor of the old infirmary was partitioned to provide service rooms, with the exception of the room at the south-east corner, which was converted into a private dining room for the abbot with a large fireplace inserted into the north wall for his comfort. The old infirmary kitchen was substantially expanded to serve this new house, with two great fireplaces and an oven in its north wall and a scullery on the south side, supplied with piped water. To the east, the old infirmarer's house was converted to become a bakehouse and brewhouse, again supplying the abbot's residence, probably with bread and ale of better quality than that received by the rest of the community.

For the few old and sick monks, a new, smaller infirmary was built to the north-east of the bakehouse and brewhouse. It lies near the modern museum.

Above: The rebus, or heraldic device, of Abbot Burton, which once adorned the abbot's house. The eagle of St John, an allusion to his first name, is carved above a tun (barrel), a reference to the final syllable of his surname

Below: A cutaway reconstruction of the infirmary hall viewed from the south-east, showing how it probably looked in the late 12th century

26 TANNERY

Most monasteries had a tannery but very few have survived. At Rievaulx, the southern end of the dormitory range was partially demolished in the late 14th century and its ground-floor room had become the abbey's tannery by the early 16th

century at a time when the government required that monastic tanneries were leased to laymen, because they were remarkably profitable operations and greatly desired by outsiders who had lobbied for them. Tile-built tanning vats were built along the west wall, supplied with water from the abbey's piped supply and discharging into the adjacent latrine drain. Two further tanning pits, originally lined with timber, also survive in the floor of the room. Tanning was a noxious process because hides were soaked in urine to remove the hairs and break down the fat, and the abbey must have reeked of the stench; by this time, however, the much reduced community would not have been using any nearby buildings.

To the west and south of the tannery and set around a small yard, all recorded in documents of 1538–9, were the tanner's house, his bark mill, lime kiln and barn, the corner of which is still visible in the site boundary.

Left: These tanning vats, in the south end of the east range, were used in the early 16th century for tanning leather, at a time when the monks were increasing their income from industrial activity
Below left: *The carved panel above the door of the later abbot's house, representing the Annunciation to the Virgin*
Below: *Manuscript depicting a very similar Annunciation scene to the one above the abbot's house at Rievaulx, from the Bolton Hours, c.1410*

Rievaulx's Last Great Patron: Abbot John Burton

John Burton was abbot of Rievaulx between 1490 and 1510. He carried out significant building works at Rievaulx and was an efficient administrator of the abbey's estates, granting or renewing the leases of several tenants. The abbot also performed services for the local church and gentry.

During his rule, Rievaulx played a key role in the religious life of the local community. In his will of 1510, the local gentleman John Clervaux made Burton his chief executor and requested burial before the image of Our Lady at the entrance to the choir at Rievaulx. Clervaux also bequeathed his amber rosary and four gold nobles (a high value coin) to the abbot in return for his prayers.

Burton was a patron of his monastery's art and architecture. It is likely that the nave of the church was remodelled during his rule. These works must have been expensive. Burton obtained extra income when he received permission from Pope Alexander VI in 1497 to hold a benefice, a right to revenue from church property normally reserved for a parish priest 'to enable him to be maintained in abbatial dignity'. Burton converted the abbey's former infirmary into a palatial lodging, which he ornamented with his rebus: the eagle of St John, an allusion to his first name, above a tun (barrel), a reference to the final syllable of his surname (see page 26). He also used the ornament of his

lodging to assert his devotion to the Virgin. Above the entrance is an image of the Annunciation to the Virgin. Its location is a reference to the belief that the gates of heaven, slammed shut at the Fall of Adam and Eve, were miraculously reopened by the Virgin's humility at the Incarnation.

Right: A plan of the valley, showing both surviving and vanished features of the monastic precinct. To extend the precinct, the community modified a number of topographic features in the valley

1 *The river Rye, whose course was diverted, nearly doubling the monastery's meadow land and allowing for the construction of buildings for the outer court*

2 *Original course of the river Rye, which once flowed through the centre of the valley, as indicated by the blue dots*

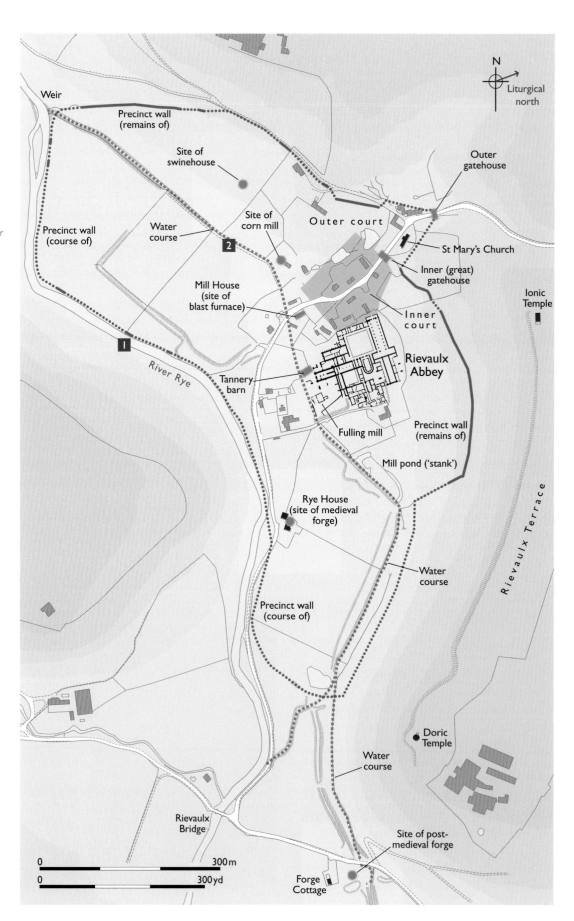

PRECINCT AND SURROUNDINGS

The buildings now in the care of English Heritage represent only the nucleus of the medieval abbey. The church and cloister ranges lay at the centre of a walled precinct of some 37ha (92 acres), within which the monks cleared the trees and created closes for livestock, agricultural buildings, industrial areas, orchards, gardens and guest houses. They organized the different enterprises so as to prevent the more intrusive functions from disturbing the monks' ordered routine.

The precinct was divided into the inner and outer courts, with access to each controlled by a gatehouse. The principal entrance to the abbey lay on the north side. All the buildings of the inner court lie under the present village, but their purposes are known from Suppression-period documents: the guest hall, bakehouse, brewhouse, kiln house, the 'house at the parlour door' and a stable.

Outer Court

The outer court, for agricultural and industrial work, fell into three parts. On the west side (following monastic directions) lay the great swinehouse, corn mill (north of the water channel) and common stable. To the south was the tannery (which used the end of the great east range), with the associated bark mill, lime house and tanners' house nearby. East of these buildings was the abbey's fulling mill, where woollen cloth was bleached and wool stored for export. Further south-east was a water-powered forge, with a large pond or 'stank' associated with it. Other areas of the precinct were drained to create water meadows.

Some of these features are still visible today. Parts of the stone wall that surrounded the precinct survive, in varying conditions. Although little of the inner or outer courts survives, the road into the village from the north-west passes through the sites of both gatehouses. Parts of the inner or great gatehouse can be seen on either side of the road immediately below the church, which incorporates the remains of the gatehouse chapel. South of the monastic buildings, part of the tannery barn is visible in the boundary wall, while the remains of the fulling mill lie near the path between the abbey and visitor centre. The 'stank', or large pond, can be seen east of the museum.

Between 1920 and 1950, when the ruins were cleared, many thousands of tonnes of debris were

spread over nearby fields; mounds still remain to the south and east of the site as a result of this dumping of rubble. Other mounds are the remains of slag heaps which date from the post-Suppression period. At this period the village of Rievaulx began to develop around the great gatehouse: several cottages, some still thatched, date from this time, and were built with stone taken from the remains of the abbey.

Above: An early 14th-century stone frieze from the infirmary hall, depicting a donkey laden with corn being taken to a mill

Below: The abbey seen from Rievaulx Terrace, which is managed by the National Trust

History of the Abbey

BIRTH OF THE CISTERCIAN ORDER

Monastic life expanded dramatically in the late 11th century. New religious orders were born at this time, each offering its own model for communal living. One such was the reform order which originated at Cîteaux in Burgundy, eastern France, in 1098, whose monks are known as Cistercians. Their intention was to adhere more closely to the *Rule of St Benedict* – the blueprint for monastic life, written in the 540s, and the foundation document of all western monasticism. They also wished to follow the example of the Apostles, who lived together in Jerusalem after Christ's death and Resurrection.

After surviving difficult early years, the Cîteaux founders were joined in 1112 by 30 more men, a number of whom were from the knightly classes. They included Bernard of Fontaines, the future saint. The increase stretched Cîteaux's resources and led to the establishment of a daughter house or satellite monastery at La Ferté, also in Burgundy, in 1113. Three more monasteries were started in quick succession, including that at Clairvaux, in the Champagne, with the 25-year-old Bernard as abbot. These five became known as the mother houses of the order. By 1119 there were 10 Cistercian monasteries, and Pope Callixtus II – who had previously been Archbishop of Vienne in Burgundy, and therefore knew the new movement well – recognized the Cistercians as a new order.

Thereafter, the growth of the order was without parallel in the history of monasticism. By 1150 more than 330 abbeys had been founded throughout Europe, and by 1200 the number had reached 525. These were communities for men; similarly extensive were those for women. Why communal living exercised an appeal on this scale is still not fully understood. Part of the explanation lies in the period's novel definition of the individual's likeness to God and the manner in which this was shared by others.

The Cistercians' success derived from a radical simplification of monastic practice and from their willingness to open monastic life to wider social groups. Simplification carried an appeal through a return to the basic principles of disciplined communal life outlined in the *Rule of St Benedict* and directed towards a life of prayer, praise and work. For the upper classes the Cistercians shaped their movement to accord with the period's chivalric ideals, calling their monks the 'new soldiers of Christ'. They also opened religious life, for the first time in monastic history, to the labouring and uneducated classes, by introducing a new category known as the lay brothers (*conversi* in Latin). The difference between the monks and lay brothers was identified in dress. The monks wore undyed or white habits, in studied contrast to the black worn by monks of the other orders, and came to be commonly known as the 'white monks', while the lay brothers wore brown habits and were also allowed beards.

Insisting on poverty and simplicity of life, and requiring manual labour from everyone, the Cistercians presented a model which, when allied to their spiritual ideals and discipline, carried wide appeal. Most of the agricultural labour on monastic farms, known as granges, was carried out by the lay brothers, who returned to the abbey on Sundays and feast days. They also shouldered the light industrial work within the precinct. They took monastic vows but these were less demanding than those of the monks, who spent much more of their day in study and prayer.

The life of both monks and lay brothers was austere and often harsh. Discipline was exacting, the regime unrelenting, the workload excessive, the diet simple and vegetarian. Nevertheless, in an age notable for its roughness and instability, a great institution like Rievaulx offered a highly structured, dedicated life providing, in the words of Aelred, 'everywhere peace, everywhere serenity, and a marvellous freedom from the tumult of the world'.

Below: In this 13th-century manuscript illustration, Stephen Harding (on the left), one of the leaders of the Cistercian movement, dispatches a group of monks to found new abbeys

Facing page: Detail from Riders Pausing by the Ruins of Rievaulx Abbey by John Wootton, c.1740–50

'In your land there is an outpost of my Lord and your Lord ... I have proposed to occupy it and I am sending men from my army who will, if it is not displeasing to you, claim it, recover it, and restore it with a strong hand.'
Bernard of Clairvaux, writing to Henry I about Rievaulx, 1131

THE FOUNDATION OF RIEVAULX

More than 80 Cistercian monasteries were founded in the British Isles, beginning in 1128 with the settlement of Waverley in Surrey. Three years later, Rievaulx was established – the first Cistercian community in the north of England.

For their monasteries, the new monks deliberately sought land in isolated areas. Such land was cheaper and therefore more likely to be given by donors. Remoteness also reduced the risk of litigation from neighbours or episcopal control and made it easier to enforce seclusion and strict enclosure. In the early 12th century few people lived on the North York moors, and there were even fewer monasteries. When the Domesday survey was made in 1086 only three religious houses were listed; by the time of Rievaulx's foundation in 1132 the number had grown to nine; and by the mid 12th century to 30.

Rievaulx was launched with the deliberate intention of making it the centre of Cistercian reform in the north. Its patron was Walter Espec, lord of Helmsley, a royal justiciar, vassal of Henry I of England and David I of Scotland, and a wealthy landowner. He was also an active supporter of ecclesiastical reform. The establishment of Rievaulx sent a shockwave through older monastic communities in the north and sparked calls for reform. An immediate effect was felt at St Mary's

Abbey, York, a traditional Benedictine house. Within months, a group of monks and the prior had left St Mary's to found another Cistercian house at Fountains Abbey near Ripon, south-west of Rievaulx.

The original gift of land from Espec, 2 miles from his castle at Helmsley, comprised about 405ha (1,000 acres). The estate ranged from arable lands to those in the deep valley of the river Rye, which gives its name to the abbey: Rye (Rie) and vaulx (valley). Some months before the founding community arrived, an advance party of monks and lay brothers chose a roughly shaped ridge on the valley's steep west-facing side, regularized it to form a terrace and raised on it the temporary wooden buildings which the order required before the monks could settle. The site was probably close to the present cloister, where modern geophysical surveying has revealed the remains of earlier buildings below ground. The choice was shrewd. The site offers warmth and a degree of shelter in summer, although it forms a frost hollow in winter. It also provided excellent and accessible freshwater springs for drinking, drainage and power, as well as good building stone.

Rievaulx's founding monastery was Clairvaux in eastern France. To help launch the new community its abbot, Bernard, wrote to Henry I to enlist his support (see quote, left). His words reveal an

Above: A 12th-century illustration of St Bernard, abbot of Clairvaux, who was the most influential churchman of his day
Right: The abbey church, seen from the infirmary cloister. The abbey was founded in the early 12th century in a deliberately remote location

Building the Abbey

Most of the stone used to build the abbey came from local quarries.

The abbey was mainly built of sandstone which came from a variety of quarries within a radius of about 10 miles. With relatively few roads in the Middle Ages, transportation was a critical element in building. Analysis of the stone used at Rievaulx shows six or seven quarry locations in Ryedale and Bilsdale. Some specially imported stone for ornamental purposes came from much further afield, such as the Frosterley marble used for detailing in the choir, which came from around Weardale, County Durham. Certain stone was favoured in different periods, although other factors such as the abbey's ownership of land, the quality of the stone, or the type of building being constructed were also important.

The earliest quarry exploited by the monks, known as Rievaulx Bank, lay uphill just 100m (103yds) north of the cloister. This yielded a very tough stone which could only be roughly hammered into shape. Within a few years, an alternative, fine-grained, yellowish-brown sandstone was being worked at the Penny Piece quarry just west of the precinct. Though also difficult to shape, this was used extensively as rubble fill for the walls throughout the abbey's building history.

By far the largest source of stone came from the Wethercote quarries 6 miles north of Rievaulx. A conservative estimate indicates that more than 90,000 tonnes of stone was quarried here. The stone was dressed at the quarry site and traces remain there of the medieval tool marks and dressing floors, together with large quantities of waste material and rejected sandstone blocks. Fairly gently inclined trackways between the quarry

and the abbey, still identifiable in parts, facilitated transport. The good quality, pale brown sandstone from here could be carved into large pieces for piers, capitals and footings as well as for squared ashlar blocks.

For the highest quality stone found in the late 12th-century refectory and early 13th-century choir, the monks used a fine-grained oolite limestone containing about 20 per cent quartz from the Griff Bank quarries, about 1 mile south-east of the abbey. Pale brown when cut and weathering to near cream white, this could take finely detailed carving.

Left: The locations of the quarries which provided the stone for the abbey. Pre-Roman to medieval tracks are also shown

1 *Rievaulx Bank*
The earliest quarry used by the monks, providing Lower Calcareous grit

2 *Penny Piece*
Provided a fine-grained, Middle Jurassic sandstone, yellowish-brown in colour

3 *Wethercote*
The main source of stone, providing good quality, pale brown sandstone

4 *Laskill Grange and*
5 *Firth Bank*
Provided a similar sandstone to Wethercote

6 *Griff Bank*
Supplied the highest quality, fine-grained limestone

7 *Hollins Wood*
Provided a fine, soft sandstone used for the detailed sculpture in some late 12th-century building

Left: A limestone frieze, originally from the infirmary hall, depicting the theft of a tiger cub from its mother

Above: A 13th-century carved boss, depicting the Agnus Dei, *the Lamb of God, which was originally from Abbot William's shrine*

Below: The remains of Abbot William's shrine, which stands between the main and north entrances to the chapter house

Below right: A reconstruction drawing of Abbot William's shrine, based on excavation evidence, showing the shrine from the cloister alley, where it had a triangular pedimented gable

identity quite different from the one we associate with monks in the 21st century: the new monastery was conceived as a kind of corps of soldiers, and the early Cistercians saw themselves as a spiritualized militia. The monks were to establish Rievaulx as an outpost from which further colonies were to be sent out with the goal of claiming the north. The new monastery was part mission centre, part headquarters, part economic regenerator. This model was combined with a determined religious faith, and the combination proved attractive to many men.

EARLIEST YEARS

Heading the new community at Rievaulx was Abbot William, a native Yorkshireman who had been educated in York. In about 1118 he learned of the new reform movement in France and travelled to join the three-year-old community at Clairvaux. After 15 years there, during which he rose to become Bernard's secretary, William was chosen to lead the new settlement at Rievaulx.

Under William's direction, Rievaulx expanded. From the founding community of about 30 men, more than 300 are mentioned at the time of William's death 13 years later. To his spiritual gifts, which earned him the title *beatus* (blessed), he

added formidable business and managerial skills. Both were essential to enlarge the abbey's lands and attract new patrons. He was also responsible for constructing the first buildings in stone, including the standing parts of the west range. These indicate a scale for the new abbey corresponding to the present buildings around the cloister.

At his death in 1145 William was buried in the chapter house. His cult grew steadily, leading the community a century later to construct a shrine to him in the left opening of the building's entry doorway. This meant that it could be used both from the cloister (for lay veneration on occasion) and from the interior of the chapter house (for the community). William's feast day was celebrated on 2 August.

William's successor was Maurice, who had joined Rievaulx from the Benedictine community at Durham, where he had been sub-prior. A scholar more than an administrator, he resigned his office after 18 months. One notable achievement, however, involved his negotiation of additional land within the valley of the Rye. When Rievaulx was founded, the land on the opposite (Ashberry Hill) side of the valley was owned by the monks of Old Byland, who belonged to a rival monastic order, the Savigniacs; their first buildings lay a mile

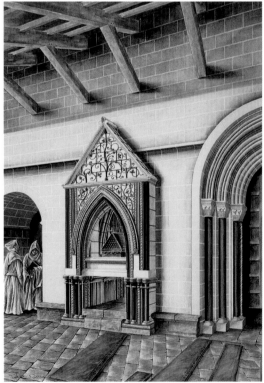

upstream. Since the two monasteries followed slightly different timetables, their bells disturbed each other, creating a situation 'which was not fitting and could not be endured'. After a number of meetings, the Old Byland monks withdrew their claim to the land and in 1147 agreed to move to a new site, at about the same time that the Cistercian order absorbed the Savigniacs. The agreement left the Rievaulx monks in sole possession of the entire valley and gave them about 30 per cent more land within the precinct.

AELRED AND EXPANSION

Two years after the abbey's foundation, William admitted a new recruit, Aelred, who was destined to become Rievaulx's most famous figure. After joining Rievaulx in 1134, Aelred worked his way up the monastery's hierarchy quickly, taking up the office of novice master in 1142, travelling to Rome to the papal court in the same year, and being appointed founder abbot of Revesby in Lincolnshire, one of Rievaulx's daughter houses,

in 1143. Four years later, aged 37, he became abbot of Rievaulx, a position he was to hold for the next 20 years.

Aelred's fame drew many men to Rievaulx. During his abbacy, the size of the community doubled, peaking in the early 1160s at about 650 men. With these numbers Rievaulx also founded new daughter monasteries, many in the north of England and the south of Scotland which, in turn, founded daughter houses; 100 years later, it had 19 dependent abbeys in total. To accommodate the increased numbers at Rievaulx, Aelred constructed larger buildings during his 20-year rule of which many remain, and he emerges as one of the great builder abbots of the 12th century. The architecture displays many qualities associated with the Cistercians, but it also reveals Aelred's own tastes and background. These were informed by extensive travel: scholars estimate that he was away from Rievaulx for about three months of every year, fulfilling demands for his gifts as preacher, diplomat and conciliator.

Above: Jet and bone chess pieces, dating from the 11th to 12th centuries, found at Rievaulx
Below: The magnificent 13th-century east end, with the infirmary chapel and the later abbot's lodging in the foreground

The Abbey's Estates

Rievaulx's estates were vital to the success of the monastery.

From their earliest days the Cistercians insisted that their abbeys should be self-sufficient, rather than live off rents, tithes and feudal services, as other orders did. To achieve this, the monks engaged in a wide range of tasks, such as milling, tanning, shoe and cloth making and brewing inside the precinct. Outside the precinct they controlled fisheries, worked mines and quarries, bred horses and cattle, practised agriculture and earned a reputation for water control and management.

Central to their economy was the creation of the grange or estate farm. At its height Rievaulx had about 20 granges, which varied between 150 and 200ha (370–500 acres) in size. These lay mostly to the north or north-east and centred on the home granges of Griff, Newlass, Bilsdale, Laskill and Sproxton. Granges produced cereal crops to supply the abbey and raised cattle. More than half the abbey's land was meadow or common pasture, principally for raising sheep. When the Crown confiscated one year's wool clip as the Cistercian order's contribution towards the ransom of King Richard I in 1193 (when he was being held captive in Germany), wool was described as 'the chief part of their [the Cistercians'] substance'.

In the early days of the order, up to 20 lay brothers would man a grange, returning to Rievaulx for Sundays and feast days. By about 1300, however, the lay brotherhood had disappeared completely, and for the last 200 years of its life, Rievaulx – in common with other Cistercian monasteries – resorted to a different economic model. The order's original notion of self-sufficiency gave way to estate management: the abbey rented out its lands, and put in tenants to run the granges.

Above: A monk-cellarer tasting wine from a barrel, from a late 13th-century French manuscript. The monks at Rievaulx were self-sufficient and would have brewed their own ale

Above right: Cistercian lay brothers cutting down a tree, from a late 13th-century manuscript

Right: A map showing Rievaulx's granges in the early 14th century

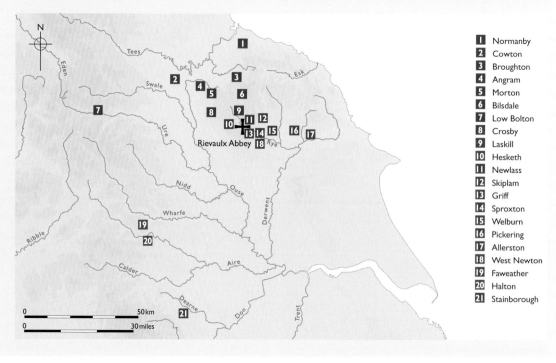

1. Normanby
2. Cowton
3. Broughton
4. Angram
5. Morton
6. Bilsdale
7. Low Bolton
8. Crosby
9. Laskill
10. Hesketh
11. Newlass
12. Skiplam
13. Griff
14. Sproxton
15. Welburn
16. Pickering
17. Allerston
18. West Newton
19. Faweather
20. Halton
21. Stainborough

AELRED'S LAST YEARS AND LEGACY

Aelred's last years were clouded by illness. His biographer, Walter Daniel, who was the infirmary master at Rievaulx, described his ailments so precisely that modern doctors can diagnose the principal problems as osteoarthritis and kidney and urinary stones. Walter Daniel tells us that, during bouts of severe illness, Aelred was in such pain that he was reduced to lying on the ground in front of a fire 'twisted in pain like a sheet of parchment'; his skin became so sensitive to touch that it required a man at each corner of a sheet to carry him to relieve himself, or to the baths to reduce his suffering from inflammation. Daniel's account also provides a rare human picture of Aelred and explains why the order exceptionally allowed him to live in separate accommodation adjacent to the dormitory, rather than sleep in the same space as his monks.

After his death on 12 January 1167 Aelred was buried next to Abbot William. Like William, Aelred was soon venerated. The Church also granted him the status of a *beatus* and his feast day is still observed on 12 January. None of his successors was to achieve the same renown. In his day, as well as being famed for his tolerance and psychological insight, Aelred enjoyed a reputation as a brilliant writer and is regarded as one of England's most revered biblical scholars and Latin stylists. He was also renowned as a pastoral master. Some of his books are still studied in the 21st century as exemplars for communal living (see feature, page 13).

Above left: A sick man receiving the sacrament, from a 14th-century English Cistercian manuscript, the Omne Bonum

Left: A reconstruction of the abbey viewed from the south-east in the mid 12th century, when it was at the height of its popularity under Aelred. At this date the west and east ranges had reached their fullest extent

RIEVAULX IN THE LATER MIDDLE AGES

Because no chronicle survives, and because Cistercian abbeys were exempt from visitation by diocesan bishops, very little is known of the history of Rievaulx after the death of Aelred. Although the community thinned, Rievaulx's appeal seems to have been sustained for much of the next century, along with that of the neighbouring Cistercian monasteries of Byland and Fountains (each with several hundred men). Large additional buildings were raised and the church was extended spectacularly in the 1220s, probably to provide space for the shrine and cult of Aelred.

The Cistercians had enjoyed wide support in the 12th century. After that, however, with the rise of town-based monastic movements, particularly the Franciscan and Dominican friars, they found themselves competing for both patronage and new recruits. Other factors – economic, educational and spiritual – had also changed. The gradual fall in the number of monks at Rievaulx reflects these new realities. Whereas at the peak of its popularity in the mid 12th century the abbey was home to as many as 650 men – monks, lay brothers and servants – 100 years later the community had shrunk to half this size. By the time of the Suppression in 1538 numbers had dwindled further to about 125 men, of whom only 23 were monks. To see this as decline simplifies what was, in fact, a complex change in the perception at that time of how best to follow a religious vocation.

As the order developed, the Cistercians had to contend with internal and external tensions. One such centred on the issue of equality. From the early days, the division of the monastery between the monks and the lay brothers carried the risk of hardening into two distinct social classes. The lay brothers, who performed most of the manual work, believed that they should share in decisions and in the election of abbots. Friction led to the exclusion of the lay brothers from the cloister and to changes to their buildings. Over time, their numbers decreased, and substitute labour had to be hired.

Dramatic economic reverses darkened the last quarter of the 13th century. A document dated 1275 records a picture of prosperity at Rievaulx, with the wool clip of that year indicating a flock of about 14,000 sheep. Reliance on wool as the major source of income, however, carried high risks, particularly when it was linked to the practice of selling it on forward contracts.

The Sacking of Rievaulx

Rievaulx's peace and tranquillity were shattered in the autumn of 1322 when war between England and Scotland brutally intruded into the paradise of the cloister.

The Scots invaded northern England and on 14 October 1322 defeated the English army at the Battle of Scawton Moor, also known as the Battle of Byland. Edward II was sitting down to a fine dinner at Rievaulx when he heard news of the defeat and hurriedly fled the abbey, narrowly escaping capture by the Scots.

The king abandoned the royal treasure at Rievaulx, which was seized by the victorious Scots. The abbey was also pillaged. A contemporary annotation in a manuscript from the abbey's library records that on the feast of St Callixtus (14 October) 1322 the Scots despoiled and damaged Rievaulx, carrying away 'books, chalices and the sacred ornaments of the monastery'.

A harness pendant (above) emblazoned with the arms of Edward II, excavated at Rievaulx and on display in the museum, is a tangible reminder of this violent episode in Rievaulx's history.

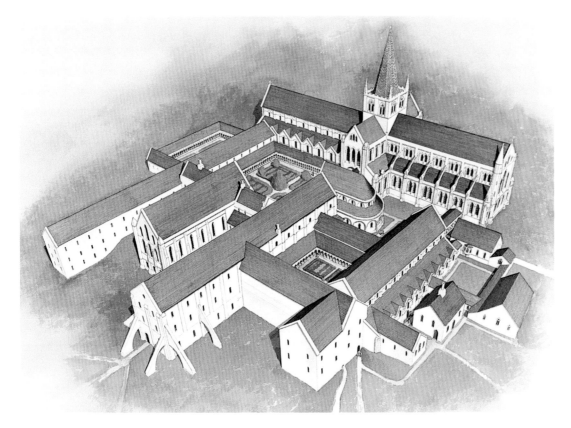

The following year an epidemic of murrain or scab decimated the abbey's sheep. Subsequent outbreaks of the disease led to bankruptcy, and by 1279 King Edward I was forced to intervene and install an external financial administrator. The community was eventually dispersed to other houses. When it was reassembled, the scale of the economic collapse was clear: in 1301 only 30 lay brothers are recorded at Rievaulx and its granges.

Agricultural and economic calamity was compounded by war and disease. King Edward II was staying at Rievaulx in 1322 when his army was surprised by the Scots and defeated by them at the Battle of Byland. The English retreated to York and the Scots plundered Rievaulx before they withdrew (see feature, opposite). The extent of the damage they caused is unknown. Two decades later the deadly plague known as the Black Death swept through the north. These setbacks had a dramatic effect on Rievaulx – by the 1370s the community numbered only 15 monks and three lay brothers.

To survive such times, the monks broke up the abbey's granges and rented out their lands. Forty-nine tenant farmers are noted in the early 15th century. Some of the monastic buildings

were demolished and others remodelled, reflecting the reduced size of the community. A partial recovery followed. Just before the Suppression, Rievaulx's community consisted of 23 monks and 102 'servants and attendants'. Further proof of revived conditions is evident from increased income from tenanted lands and also from industrial activity, both of which provided money for the monks to fund building renovations to the abbot's house, improvements to their church, adaptations to the cloister buildings and changes to the industrial buildings in the outer court.

Above left: A reconstruction showing the main abbey buildings viewed from the south-east in about 1250. By this time the east end had been extended and a tall tower with a spire inserted over the crossing. The refectory had been turned at right angles to the cloister alley. Giant flying buttresses had been built to offset subsidence of the east range

Above: A fragment of 14th-century glass decorated with a crowned letter 'J'

Left: An illustration of a couple stricken by the Black Death from the Toggenburg Bible, 1411. The Black Death swept through northern England in the mid 14th century and by the 1370s the community at Rievaulx was dramatically reduced in size

THE END OF MONASTIC LIFE

In 1530, the community elected Edward Kirby as its 37th abbot. A conservative churchman, he was perhaps not the best choice, for the Church in England was about to undergo major change as Henry VIII (r.1509–47) broke with Rome when the Pope failed to annul his marriage to Catherine of Aragon. In 1532, Henry declared himself supreme head, below God, of the Church in England, and in the following years began to apply great pressure on monastic institutions. At Rievaulx, Abbot Kirby was deprived of his office in 1533 for questioning Henry's authority to interfere in church matters and Rowland Blyton was installed in his place.

In 1536 the majority of monasteries with an income of less than £200 a year were suppressed, resulting in the outbreak of a rebellion in the north known as the Pilgrimage of Grace. Henry treated this as sedition, and an excuse to close the remaining, larger monasteries, which included Rievaulx. Between 1536 and 1540 843 religious houses were closed, of which 63 were Cistercian. At Rievaulx the end came on 3 December 1538, when Abbot Blyton and 21 monks gathered in their chapter house for the last time and 'voluntarily' surrendered their monastery to the royal commissioners. The community here was luckier than at many other monasteries: the monks and abbot were awarded pensions – Abbot Blyton was also granted the house of Skiplam Grange – and the servants and attendants were paid off. After a life of 406 years, Rievaulx Abbey ceased to be a monastery.

Above right: King Henry VIII, seen here in an illuminated initial from the Valor Ecclesiasticus, *the survey of monastic property made in 1535*

Right: The abbey in about 1500. The west range, kitchen, warming house, chapter house, infirmary and east range had all been reduced in size and remodelled to reflect the reduced size of the community

The 17th-century antiquary William Dudgale records that Brother Henry Thirsk (or Cawton), a monk at Rievaulx at the time of its suppression, had read a prophecy in a manuscript belonging to the abbey that foretold its closure:

Two men came riding over Hackney way,
The one of a black horse, the other on a gray;
The one unto the other did say,
Lo, yonder stood Revess [Rievaulx], the faire abbey.

Dugdale records that when Brother Thirsk, 'or any of his fellows did read it, they used to throw the book away in anger, as thinking it impossible ever to come to pass'.

RIEVAULX AFTER THE SUPPRESSION

Immediately after the Suppression, the lands and home estates in Bilsdale and Raisdale were sold to Thomas Manners, 1st Earl of Rutland (d.1543), who was closely associated with the royal court. To ensure an orderly process of disposal, and to avoid the mob ransacking that had occurred at other monasteries, Rutland had three inventories made in the first 12 months after the monks surrendered the abbey. Two documents in

particular – the first inventory, which lists the buildings' contents and fittings, and a survey made in the course of demolition, which identifies the use of 76 individual buildings – provide an exceptionally clear picture of late Cistercian life.

Above: A lead fother with the royal stamp, 1538–9, made from lead melted down from the roof of the abbey church
Left: Effigies of Thomas Manners, 1st Earl of Rutland, who bought Rievaulx Abbey after the Suppression, and his wife, in the Church of St Mary at Bottesford, Leicestershire

The Suppression Inventories

When the site of the abbey was granted to the Earl of Rutland in 1538, little or no demolition had taken place. The responsibility for that was left to its new owner, though the king as usual retained most of the roof leads and bells. The process of breaking up the abbey and its home estate was recorded by Rutland's steward at Helmsley, Ralf Bawde, in an exceptional series of documents that survive at Belvoir Castle. From them we learn about the furnishing of the church and abbot's house, the use of many buildings before the Suppression and the location of some 25 lost buildings beyond the

cloister, including the tannery and three mills.

The inventories describe the high altar with a screen behind it, its gilded wooden frontal and altarpiece with a gilded statue of Our Lady, ten other gilded 'images' and a little gilded shrine above the altar, all then still in place. The records suggest, however, that the crossing

tower had already fallen, because the transept roof was 'all to brokyn with the falling of the steple', and the floor of the south transept was covered with fallen timbers and lead, together with the bells and bell-frame. It also appears that William Blythman of the Court of Augmentations had taken away things he was not entitled

to, including half of the monks' desks or carrels in the cloister that had already been offered to one George Lee. The roof timbers of the cloister, however, were reserved for burning down and casting the king's lead.

Below: Detail of a woodcut from John Foxe's 'Book of Martyrs', showing a church being ransacked

Right: Fragment of stonework from the abbey, reset in the wall of St Mary's Church, Rievaulx. The inscription reads: [Abba]s Rievall[is] and probably comes from an early 14th-century abbatial grave slab in the chapter house

Below right: This drawing of a water-powered blast furnace, made in about 1580, shows what the furnace at Rievaulx, built at about the same time, may have looked like

They also ensure that we know more about the process by which the abbey was dismantled and its contents dispersed than about any other English abbey (see page 41).

The Earl of Rutland directed his 'fierce aggression', in the words of a contemporary, towards the destruction of the buildings making up the core of the monastery. Only the old infirmary, newly remodelled as the abbot's residence in the early 16th century, was left intact (see page 26). Rutland clearly attempted to make the most of his investment: he sold the roof timbers and fittings, and divided the window glass into three categories: the best quality was to be kept, the second to be sold and the poorest taken from its leads and the lead recovered.

Within the outer court were a number of houses occupied by pensioners and servants of the abbey, essentially tied accommodation. In 1539, the occupants were obliged to pay rent for the first time. These buildings, together with others in the inner court, were to become part of the village of Rievaulx that succeeded the abbey. Outside the old monastic nucleus, the

Iron Production at Rievaulx

Rievaulx had been involved in iron smelting from the 1160s when it acquired estates at Fawether, Halton, Stainborough, Bingley and Shipley in South and West Yorkshire, where its bloomeries and smithies were operated in partnership with local landowners. Closer to home, iron was also worked on the home estates in Bilsdale, and at least partly processed within the precinct. Before 1538, Lambert Semer was renting and operating a water-powered smithy at Rievaulx called the Ironsmyths, the millpond of which survives in the eastern part of the precinct. This was an operation that survived the Suppression, and within a few years Rutland realized that more profit could be gained from industrial activity than from farming or rentals and he expanded the foundries, forges and mills and retained Lambert Semer.

In 1576–7 a blast furnace, its bellows driven by a waterwheel, was built – possibly the first in the north of England. The vast amounts of charcoal needed for firing the furnace were stored in the former monastic refectory. By the 1590s increased iron production required storehouses both at Rievaulx and in York. Half a century later, however, a shortage of fuel and exhaustion of the best quality iron had made the industry less profitable and industrial activity in the valley ceased.

eastern and western parts of the precinct were established as tenanted farms.

Many of the monks retained an attachment to the monastic life, salvaging property from the abbey and remembering former brethren in their wills. John Pynder Malton made his one month after the abbey was suppressed. He bequeathed vestments and a missal to Thornton parish church. The shortness of the interval between the suppression of Rievaulx and his will suggests these must come from the abbey. He also left 12d to 'everyone of my brethren late of the monastery of Revalles' to say Masses for his soul. Catholicism was restored during the reign of Mary I (r.1553–8) and a small number of monasteries were revived. Although none was Cistercian, Roland Blyton, last abbot of Rievaulx, assumed his former title as abbot of Rufford, a position he held before he was installed at Rievaulx.

Left: Portrait of Mary I by Antonio Moro, 1554. Catholicism was restored during Mary's reign and some monasteries were revived

Below: Aerial view of Rievaulx Abbey, which was mostly in ruins by the mid 16th century

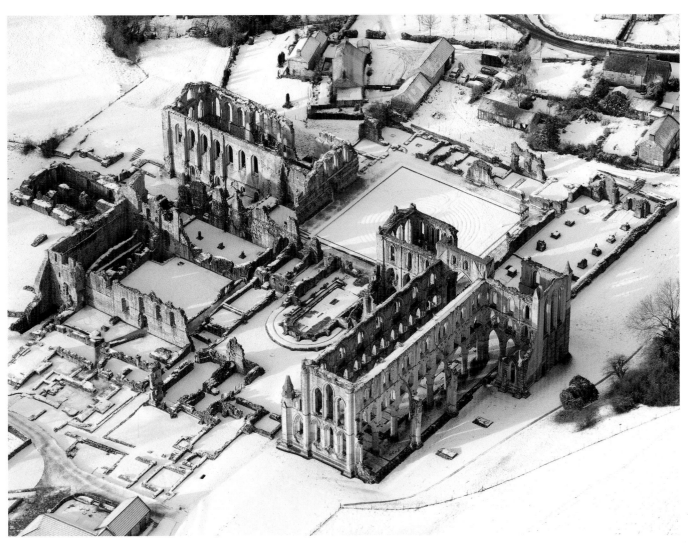

RIEVAULX AND THE PICTURESQUE

In 1695, the valley and many of the estates belonging to the former abbey were sold to Charles Duncombe (d.1711), a City of London goldsmith and banker and reputedly the richest commoner in England, for the unprecedented sum of £90,000.

His heirs, later ennobled as the earls of Feversham, commissioned a large country house and gardens outside Helmsley and named it Duncombe Park. Some years later the gardens were extended 1.5 miles northwards to link up with the valley of the Rye. Whereas the earlier gardens adhered to age-old traditions of a garden as a fenced and cultivated area linked to the house, the new layout was unfenced and extended outwards to embrace nature.

To enjoy this new approach in which the ruins played a role, guests of the Duncombes took carriages for outings to Rievaulx as early as the 1750s. Dismounting at the newly built Doric Temple, they encountered a grassed, half-mile long terrace built along the escarpment of the valley. Nine allées cut at intervals down the treed slopes offered plunging views of the ruins 90m (300ft) below, which appeared therefore as discrete tableaux or pictures (hence the term Picturesque). The terrace terminated at the Ionic Temple where the Duncombes' servants provided a formal dinner. Learned conversation would have ensued

on subjects such as the parallels between nature and liberty, or the vicissitudes of history (sparked by the desolate remains as markers of a vanished institution). In turn, comparisons might have been drawn with France's regularized garden geometries and rigid monarchy (shortly to change at the dawn of the Enlightenment and the French Revolution).

The Rievaulx Terrace with its dramatic views offers an early example of the Picturesque landscape, England's most original and influential contribution to garden history. Managed by the National Trust, the terrace is well worth a visit.

Above: A portrait of Charles Duncombe by Michael Dahl, c.1683. The abbey estates passed to Duncombe in 1695
Above right: The Ionic Temple on Rievaulx Terrace, which affords breathtaking views over the abbey
Right: An 18th-century view of Duncombe Park from across the lake. Rievaulx Abbey became part of the Duncombe Park estate in the late 17th century

Facing page: Detail of a watercolour of Rievaulx Abbey by Thomas Girtin, 1798. The abbey was a popular subject for artists in the late 18th century

'We rode down a very steep hill to Ryvaux valley, with woods all around us. We stopped upon the bridge to look at the Abbey and again when we had crossed it. Dear Mary had never seen a ruined abbey before except Whitby.'
From Dorothy Wordsworth's Grasmere Journals, *1802*

In 1715 and again in 1745 Britain was rocked by the Jacobite rebellions, attempts by the exiled descendants of the Catholic King James II (r.1685–8) to regain the throne. The Duncombe owners of the ruins were supporters of the Protestant Hanoverian dynasty and fervent opponents of the Jacobites. The rebellions prompted the interpretation of Rievaulx in political terms, with the ruins construed as a reminder of the supposed corruption, tyranny and superstition of Catholicism. Bullet holes in the south wall of the refectory and the east end of the church are the result of soldiers using the 'popish' ruin as target practice.

The success of Rievaulx's artful setting was apparent from the 1770s, when writers and artists came to the abbey to record the ruins and surrounding landscape as highlights of the Picturesque. From the late 18th century the abbey became a popular destination for visitors.

A further change occurred in the early 19th century, when the monastic remains came to be appreciated in their own right for their inherent qualities as architecture, rather than as reminders of the past. In 1802, William Wordsworth, his wife, Mary, and his sister, Dorothy, made visits to Rievaulx, one of which was on William and Mary's wedding day. Like the Duncombes' guests they viewed the ruins from 'above', but unlike them they also went down into the valley, at Dorothy's insistence, to examine the standing remains from 'below'. The shift in focus reflects a shift in attitude. From 'memory prompter', the ruins were now seen as an attraction on their own account. The enquiring Wordsworths represent a new social class of visitor approaching the physical remains with questions at far remove from the literary and philosophic musings of the Duncombes.

Efforts were also made to record and to preserve the ruins. In 1819 Thomas Whitaker wrote the first book on the surviving abbey buildings as part of a planned series on Yorkshire's monuments, of which only the Rievaulx volume materialized. In it, he deplored the crumbling condition of the abbey.

RIEVAULX AS AN ANCIENT MONUMENT

Despite the growing fame of Rievaulx, it was not until the early 20th century that the abbey became the object of professional study and consolidation. The owner, lacking the resources to repair the remains – which were in a state of imminent collapse – transferred the abbey ruins to the care of the Office of Works in 1917. The Office of Works saw the abbey as the jewel in the crown of its properties, and after the First World War Rievaulx became the model of how to present an ancient monument.

Surveys of the remains demonstrated that the east end of the church and other parts of the ruins were in danger of collapsing. Heroic measures to save the church were undertaken between 1918 and

1921 by the resourceful architect Sir Frank Baines: he devised pioneering engineering techniques, such as reinforced concrete beams hidden in the upper walls, to stabilize the building's movement. More controversial was the clearance overseen by Sir Charles Peers, who in the 1920s emptied out about 90,000 tonnes of rubble left from the Earl of Rutland's destruction. Veterans of the First World War carried out the work. Unfortunately, much excavated material was discarded and a good deal of it was either spread over adjacent fields to level them, so obscuring the medieval earthworks of the abbey, or used to build boundary walls.

Over the past 60 years changes to the site have continued. More accurate surveying and academic research have led to new discoveries in the standing remains, while study of the architectural stonework retained from the site clearance has also led to greater understanding of the sequence of building. Just as important, interest has expanded since the Second World War beyond the nucleus of monastic buildings to encompass the precinct as a whole, lying to the east and west. This area of approximately 37ha (92 acres) contained buildings and enclosures that related to the overall operation and economy of the abbey and to its granges. The study of this wider landscape has helped to illuminate the way in which the abbey worked and has given a much fuller understanding of Rievaulx's 900-year history.

RIEVAULX ABBEY HELMSLEY YORKS L·N·E·R

FULL INFORMATION FROM L·N·E·R STATIONS OFFICES AND AGENCIES

Despite this intensive research, however, much remains obscure. The earliest buildings have never been tested by excavation, although this has proved very informative elsewhere. Little is known about the inner and outer courts on the west side which relate to the entry of the monastery; buildings and landform in this area could be identified with developing methods of field survey using drones to create three-dimensional mapping. Also yet to be studied in detail is documentary evidence for the late medieval management of the abbey and its estate and this is certain to change our understanding of Rievaulx's later history.

Other changes in the last half-century have included the expansion of space to accommodate a car park. More facilities have also been created to provide services and information for increasing numbers of visitors.

Religious tolerance and ecumenism have turned attention to the abbey's medieval role as a centre of pilgrimage and to the importance of Abbot Aelred as a pastoral master and writer. As a consequence, the ruins have once more been used to hold religious services. Although it is a historical monument, the perception of Rievaulx and of its history today is far from fixed. Its story is still evolving.

Above: *Visitors to Rievaulx in about 1930*
Right: *View of the church from the south-east, seen from across the valley*